# I'm Going To READ!

These levels are meant only as guides;
you and your child can best choose a book that's right.

### Level 1: Kindergarten–Grade 1 . . . Ages 4–6
- word bank to highlight new words
- consistent placement of text to promote readability
- easy words and phrases
- simple sentences build to make simple stories
- art and design help new readers decode text

UP TO **50** WORDS

### Level 2: Grade 1 . . . Ages 6–7
- word bank to highlight new words
- rhyming texts introduced
- more difficult words, but vocabulary is still limited
- longer sentences and longer stories
- designed for easy readability

UP TO **100** WORDS

### Level 3: Grade
- richer v                        nt words
- varied
- high-inte                  plots
- designed               dependent reading

UP TO **200** WORDS

### Level 4: Grades 3 and up . . . Ages 8 and up
- richer vocabulary of more than 300 different words
- short chapters, multiple stories, or poems
- more complex plots for the newly independent reader
- emphasis on reading for meaning

MORE THAN **300** WORDS

# LEVEL 3

Library of Congress Cataloging-in-Publication Data Available

2  4  6  8  10  9  7  5  3  1

Published by Sterling Publishing Co., Inc.
387 Park Avenue South, New York, NY 10016
Text copyright © 2005 by Harriet Ziefert Inc.
Illustrations copyright © 2005 by Andrea Baruffi
Distributed in Canada by Sterling Publishing
c/o Canadian Manda Group, 165 Dufferin Street
Toronto, Ontario, Canada M6K 3H6
Distributed in Great Britain and Europe by Chris Lloyd at Orca Book
Services, Stanley House, Fleets Lane, Poole BH15 3AJ, England
Distributed in Australia by Capricorn Link (Australia) Pty. Ltd.
P.O. Box 704, Windsor, NSW 2756, Australia

I'm Going To Read is a trademark of Sterling Publishing Co., Inc.

Sterling ISBN 1-4027-2104-8

# I Won't Go to Bed!

## Pictures by Andrea Baruffi

Sterling Publishing Co., Inc.
New York

The clock said nine.
Jake should have been asleep.
But he was not.

Jake wanted to stay up
all night.

"I won't go to bed," said Jake. "I won't. I'm going to stay up all night."

"Well, I'm going to bed,"
said his father.
"I'm not staying up
all night."

Jake sat in his father's chair.
He felt big.
He felt important.

Jake switched
the television on . . .
and off.

"Nothing good on TV,
he said to no one
but himself.

"Maybe I should
read the newspaper."

After a while,
Jake sat himself
at the bottom
of the steps.

In the quiet of the night
he listened to
his father snore.

Around ten o'clock a mouse
dashed across the floor.

"Hello, mouse!"

At eleven o'clock an owl hooted.
Shadows moved along the wall.

A window rattled.
Jake shivered—just a little.

**The clock
said twelve.**

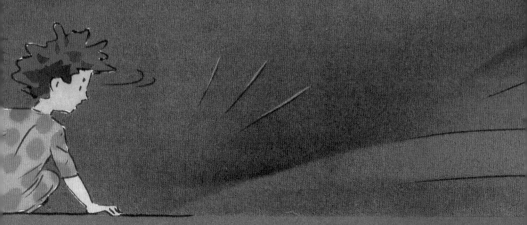

The mouse ran back
across the floor.
He looked at Jake
as if to ask,
"Why aren't you in bed?"

"I'm not going to bed,"
said Jake.
"I'm going to stay up
all night."

Jake put a blanket on the floor.
He set the table for three.
He was going to have a party!

Jake sat at the head of
the table.
He wished he could begin
the party.

But no one came.
Not even the mouse!

"So what!" said Jake.
"I can make my own party.
I'll sing!"

Jake sang
a few notes,
then stopped.

His voice sounded loud
and strange
against the quiet
of the night.

**The grandfather's clock chimed.**

**Jake was lonely.
And tired.
And bored.**

**He made himself a bed
on the floor.**

"I'm not going
to sleep," he said.
"I'm just going to take
a little rest."

While Jake slept,
night was turning into day.

Jake's father came
down the stairs.

Jake's dad patted him
gently on the head.

"Would you like me
to help you upstairs
to your bed?"
he asked.

Jake nodded yes.

Together they
went upstairs . . .

to sleep
until morning.